Ancient Egypt

500 Interesting Facts About Egyptian History

Table of Contents

Introduction 1
Predynastic Egypt (Before 3100 BCE) 2
The Unification of Upper and Lower Egypt (3100 BCE) 5
The Old Kingdom of Egypt (2686-2181 BCE) 8
The First Intermediate Period in Egypt (2181-2055 BCE) 11
The Middle Kingdom of Egypt (2055-1650 BCE) 14
The Second Intermediate Period in Egypt (1650-1550 BCE) 18
The New Kingdom of Egypt (1550-1070 BCE) 21
The Third Intermediate Period in Egypt (1070-664 BCE) 24
The Late Period in Egypt (664-332 BCE) 27
The Persian Period in Egypt (525-404 and 343-332 BCE) 30
Alexander the Great in Egypt (332-323 BCE) 32
The Ptolemaic Period in Egypt (305-30 BCE) 35
The Rise of the Pharaohs in Ancient Egypt 38
Religion and Gods in Ancient Egypt 39
Pyramids and Tombs in Ancient Egypt 40
Geography and Climate in Ancient Egypt 41
Writing and Hieroglyphs in ancient Egypt 42
Government and Administration in Ancient Egypt 43
The Military in Ancient Egypt 44
Economy and Trade in Ancient Egypt 45
Art and Architecture in Ancient Egypt 46
Literature and Poetry in Ancient Egypt 47
Science and Technology in Ancient Egypt 48
Social Structure and Roles in Ancient Egypt 49
Clothing and Appearance in Ancient Egypt 50
Farming and Agriculture in Ancient Egypt 51
Medicine and Health in Ancient Egypt 52
Death and Burial in Ancient Egypt 53
Conclusion 54
Sources and Additional References 56

Introduction

The ancient land of Egypt has long been a source of mystery and fascination, with its grand monuments, enigmatic hieroglyphs, powerful pharaohs, and colorful culture. For thousands of years, it was one of the most advanced civilizations in the world. But what do we really know about this mysterious place?
In this book, you will discover many aspects of life during this incredible time. Through vivid descriptions and detailed accounts of archaeological discoveries, you'll explore everything from religion to art to economics, uncovering secrets that have remained hidden for centuries. You'll learn how Upper and Lower Egypt unified around 3100 BCE to form one kingdom under the legendary King Menes.

We'll take a look at some distinctive features of ancient Egypt, such as the pyramids and tombs built by highly skilled masons. We will explore gods like Ra or Osiris. And we will learn about where farmers grew crops.
We'll also explore how the government, military, and economy functioned; how writing developed from simple pictograms to a fully formed alphabet; what kind of clothing Egyptians wore; and their impressive architecture. You will be fascinated by Egyptian literature, poetry, and science. Plus, you'll see why this civilization was so crucial to Western history with Alexander the Great's conquest in 332 BCE to Cleopatra, who famously met her fate at the age of thirty-nine.

We will explore ancient Egypt from Predynastic times to the Ptolemaic period. Uncover its secrets, and bring this captivating civilization back into the light.

Ancient Egypt

Predynastic Egypt
(Before 3100 BCE)

This chapter will explore the fascinating **history of Predynastic Egypt.** We'll look at thirty interesting facts about Egyptian beliefs, tools, art, and more. We'll discover some of the most important **Predynastic cultures** and how they contributed to society and the development of Egypt.

1. **People lived in Egypt starting around 200,000 BCE.**

2. Some scholars believe that **Homo erectus wandered through Egypt** nearly two million years ago!

3. **Predynastic Egypt tends to start around 6000 BCE**, toward the end of the Neolithic period.

4. **The people of Predynastic Egypt were hunter-gatherers and farmers** who lived in small villages along the Nile River and its tributaries.

5. **The world's earliest sickle blades were made in Egypt.** It is believed they were created sometime around 10,500 BCE.

6. **The Egyptians developed a system of irrigation to water their crops** and control the floods along the Nile River. Irrigation systems became common around 3000 BCE.

7. **Predynastic Egyptians built boat**s and used them to travel up and down the river, which helped them trade goods with other cultures nearby, like Mesopotamia.

8. As the centuries passed, **Egyptians traded** with more and more civilizations, such as Nubia.

9. **Prehistoric and Predynastic Egyptians** used stone tools to cut stones for everyday activities, such as cutting up meat and preparing animal skins.

10. **They also made jewelry** from shells, feathers, and bones.

11. **Predynastic Egyptians used copper** for many of their tools.

2

12. **Predynastic Egyptians lived in houses made of mudbricks,** which were dried in the sun.

13. Some of the earliest **art forms created in Egypt include rock paintings** on cave walls depicting animals like gazelles or hippos and drawings of humans doing everyday activities like hunting or fishing.

14. **The world's first board game, senet,** was invented in Egypt around 3500 BCE.

15. **Egypt's famous writing system** was developed right before the age of the pharaohs. **Hieroglyphics** were made up of symbols that represented objects, sounds, and ideas.

16. **Music was an important part** of prehistoric and Predynastic Egypt. Music played a crucial role in rituals and burials.

17. **Weaving was first used** during the Faiyum A culture (9000–6000 BCE).

18. **The first faience** (fine tin-glazed pottery) was first made during the Predynastic period.

19. **Prehistoric and Predynastic Egyptians** made simple clay figures of people, animals, and gods.

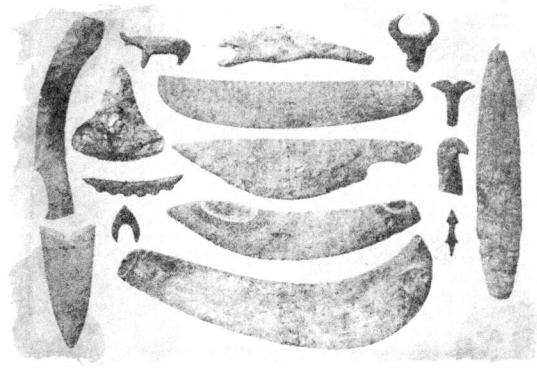

20. **Pottery was initially undecorated and purely functional.** By the time of the Tasian culture, which began around 4500 BCE, pottery began to be used for ornamental purposes as well.

21. **Prehistoric and Predynastic Egyptians** worshiped a variety of gods. They were likely similar to or the same as the ones ancient Egyptians worshiped, such as Ra and Osiris.

22. **Predynastic Egyptians had mummies,** but they weren't wrapped in bandages. Instead, these bodies were likely mummified by the dry weather.

Ancient Egypt

23. **During the Naqada culture** (c. 4000–3000 BCE), the first clear evidence of elite tombs was discovered, showing the stratification of society.

24. **The Gerzean culture** (3500–3200 BCE) built the first traditional Egyptian tombs.

25. **Predynastic Egypt** wasn't a lawless place. There were rulers of Upper Egypt and Lower Egypt.

26. **Lower Egypt** is the northern part of the country near the Nile Delta, and Upper Egypt is farther south, where the land is more elevated.

27. **The use of math in Egypt** dates back to the Predynastic period. There is evidence that math was used as early as 3200 BCE!

28. **Prehistoric and Predynastic Egyptians relied on astronomy and astrology.** They used the stars to tell when the Nile would flood.

29. It is not known for sure when **the Egyptian 365-day calendar was invented,** but it was in use before the Dynastic Period (when Egypt was unified for the first time) began.

30. **Although Upper and Lower Egypt developed separately**, the two began to greatly influence each other during the time of the Tasian culture.

The Unification of Upper and Lower Egypt
(3100 BCE)

Explore the fascinating history of ancient Egypt and **the unification of Upper and Lower Egypt.** We'll look at thirty interesting facts about the ancient Egyptians' culture, beliefs, tools, and art.
Discover how the pharaohs unified the country and the advances they made in mathematics, medicine, and art.

31. **Around 3100 BCE, Egypt was unified under one ruler.**

32. Before the unification of Egypt, **Upper and Lower Egypt had its own ruler and culture.**

33. However, **the two regions shared a common language**, which allowed them to unite against foreign threats, such as invaders from Asia or Nubia.

34. **King Narmer**, whose name means "stinging catfish," is believed to have been the first pharaoh to unify Upper and Lower Egypt by conquering the northern city-states in Lower Egypt and the local rulers.

35. **King Narmer might have been the legendary King Menes.** Menes is also credited with being the first to unify Egypt.

36. To celebrate his victory over Lower Egypt, **Narmer created a ceremonial palette** in which he was depicted as a fierce lion-headed figure wearing Upper Egypt's crown and smiting his enemies with a mace. This palette is now known as **the Narmer Palette.**

37. On the other side of the Narmer Palette, **Narmer wears the crown of Lower Egypt,** signifying his rule over both regions.

38. The rulers of this unified Egypt **were called kings.** The term **pharaoh didn't appear until the New Kingdom.** (We will use pharaoh in this text as that is what rulers of ancient Egypt are commonly referred to today.)

39. Although the capital changed over time, **the first pharaohs ruled from Memphis in Lower Egypt.**

40. **The Early Dynastic period of Egypt** stretched from the unification of Egypt (3100 BCE) to around 2686 BCE, the start of the Old Kingdom.

41. **The unification of Upper and Lower Egypt** brought about new cultural changes, including a unified system of hieroglyphics for keeping records, standardized weights and measures for trading goods, and a single legal code instead of separate ones for each region.

42. After unification, **Egypt flourished economically** by trading goods like grain, oil, and papyrus paper with neighboring countries like Syria, Palestine, Nubia, and Libya for things like obsidian and gold.

43. **Papyrus paper was an incredibly important invention,** as it allowed writing to be done more quickly. Before, writing had to be carved into rock. Papyrus paper was used for centuries, and it was invented around 2900 BCE.

44. This period also saw advances in mathematical knowledge, such as geometry.

45. **Medicine greatly advanced after the unification of Egypt.** Ancient Egyptians may have believed in a form of the four "humors" (blood, phlegm, black bile, and yellow bile) or evil spirits. To treat these ailments, they used herbal remedies and spells.

46. **The idea of humors** lasted until the advent of germ theory in the 19th century.

47. **The Egyptians developed an extensive writing system called hieroglyphics** shortly before the Early Dynastic period. The use of hieroglyphics greatly expanded as time passed. Writing was used to communicate ideas such as religious beliefs, law codes, and even poetry.

48. **The Egyptian calendar** also took on more importance with the unification of Egypt. The calendar was 365 days and was divided into 12 months with 3 weeks per month (10 days each).

49. **Egyptians continued to create art**. They notably painted on the walls of their tombs, typically depicting scenes from everyday life, such as farming, hunting, or fishing.

50. **Ancient Egyptian art** was highly symbolic and held religious meaning. Images of gods and goddesses were often used to

represent ideas like fertility or protection. Other scenes depicted pharaohs performing rituals that showed their power over the people.

51. **Horus was the most important god in Early Dynastic Egypt.** Horus was the falcon-headed god and oversaw kingship and the sky.

52. **The pharaohs would come to believe that they had magical powers called heka,** which enabled them to control nature and perform miracles like bringing back the dead or controlling floods through their commands alone.

53. **Eventually, Heka became a god**. Heka was the god of medicine and magic and was quite important throughout ancient Egyptian history.

54. **Ancient Egyptians were polytheistic.** They believed in multiple gods that had different roles, such as Ra (the sun god) and Isis (the goddess of motherhood).

55. Most people know something about **the ancient Egyptian belief in the afterlife.** However, before 2000 BCE, it was believed that only pharaohs could go to the afterlife.

56. **Ancient Egypt had a complex social structure,** with pharaohs at the top, followed by priests, civil servants, and workers.

57. **Ancient Egypt had slaves,** but there is no evidence of the institution existing before the Old Kingdom period.

58. **The priesthood was formed in the Early Dynastic period** but began to take on new roles in the Old Kingdom.

59. **Priests served as intermediaries between people and gods.** They were responsible for performing rituals and ceremonies to ensure that the gods were appeased.

60. **Ancient Egypt had a series of dynasties,** each with its own pharaoh. **The pharaohs built monuments, made laws and taxes, and expanded their empire.**

Ancient Egypt

The Old Kingdom of Egypt
(2686–2181 BCE)

This chapter will explore the fascinating history of **the Old Kingdom of Egypt,** a period of ancient Egyptian civilization lasting **from 2686 to 2181 BCE**.
We will examine thirty interesting facts about their culture, beliefs, art, and architecture, from the development of hieroglyphics to the construction of **the Pyramids of Giza** and other grand monuments.
We will also explore their **belief in the afterlife**, the significance of mummification, and their sophisticated legal system based on the principle of Ma'at.

61. **The Old Kingdom** is also referred to as **the Age of Pyramids** since many pyramids were constructed during this period.

62. **Pharaohs were considered living gods** who ruled over Egypt with absolute power. Ordinary people lived in small villages or worked on farms owned by the wealthy.

63. **The ancient Egyptians had a sophisticated legal system** that was based on the principle of "Ma'at," or justice.

64. **Ma'at was also the goddess of justice and law.**

65. As mentioned above, **ancient Egyptians believed in many gods and goddesses.** During the Old Kingdom, **Ra**, the god of the sun, surpassed **Horus** as the most important god.

66. **The people visited temples** or shrines dedicated to deities to make offerings or sacrifices to gain their favor and bring good luck into their lives.

67. **Ancient Egyptian art featured bright colors** and striking imagery used to convey religious beliefs or show loyalty to pharaohs through statues and wall paintings.  Other forms of art, like jewelry making, were also very popular during this period.

68. **The Old Kingdom period** saw significant advances in literature and writing. Texts like The Instruction of Ptahhotep and the Pyramid Texts offer insight into ancient Egyptian beliefs and customs.

69. **Egypt developed an extensive network of roads** that enabled more accessible travel across the country.

70. **The Nile River was Egypt's most important geographical feature,** as it provided water for irrigation and transportation along its banks.

71. **Innovations in medicine began during the Old Kingdom.** Imhotep, a doctor, wrote down cures for diseases on papyrus scrolls, which were preserved for future generations to use.

72. **Ancient Egyptians had a very advanced medical system** which included pharmacists, surgeons, and dentists, who used natural remedies like honey to treat diseases. Some of their cures are still used today!

73. **Ancient Egyptians also made advances in mathematics, engineering, and astronomy.**

74. **The Great Sphinx** is a giant statue of a pharaoh's head on a lion's body near the Pyramids of Giza. It is believed the **Sphinx was built to protect Khafre's pyramid** (one of the Pyramids of Giza).

75. **The Great Pyramid of Giza was built by Khufu** around 2550 BCE. It is the only remaining Seven Wonder of the Ancient World.

76. **The Pyramids of Giza** were built during the Old Kingdom and are still standing today after thousands of years.

77. **The Pyramids of Giza were built as tombs for Khufu, Khafre, and Menkaure,** who wanted to be surrounded by grandeur forever.

78. **Pharaohs used richly decorated tombs** with intricate hieroglyphics inscribed on their walls to tell stories about their lives and accomplishments.

79. **The first pyramid complex was begun by Pharaoh Djoser** around 2650 BCE at Saqqara. It is known as the Step Pyramid of Djoser.

80. **In addition to the Pyramids of Giza,** the Old Kingdom was known for its immense stone monuments and other pyramid complexes **at Abusir, Saqqara, and Dahshur.** After death, ancient Egyptians believed their soul would travel through a dark tunnel and reach a bright light.

Ancient Egypt

81. Depending on how they lived on Earth, **the afterlife could be peaceful or filled with agony**.

82. **Mummification was very important to the ancient Egyptians.** They believed that the soul could only exist in a body, so mummification was a way to preserve the body from decay and ensure it could join its soul in the afterlife.

83. **Ancient Egyptians** had advanced techniques **to preserve bodies after death.** This included wrapping the body tightly in linen and burying it with items, such as food, furniture, and jewelry, that were meant for use in the afterlife.

84. **The ancient Egyptians had a government system** with a pyramid structure. Pharaohs were at the top, followed by viziers, who provided advice to pharaohs. Next came nobles who managed land or held military roles as generals or commanders. Ordinary people were at the bottom of the hierarchy above the slaves.

85. **Some professions were more respected than others.** For instance, scribes were more respected than craftsmen, but craftsmen were more respected than farmers.

86. **Slavery began during the Old Kingdom.** Most slaves were prisoners of war.

87. **The ancient Egyptians were proficient farmers** who used sophisticated methods to cultivate their crops. They had an organized agricultural year divided into three seasons: Akhet (the flooding season), Peret (the growing season), and Shemu (the harvest season).

88. It wasn't all work in ancient Egypt. **The Egyptians loved to play board games** like senet, which is still popular today. They played other board games as well, such as mehen and hounds and jackals.

89. **Board games were often found in tombs,** as they were seen as a way for people to pass the time in the afterlife.

90. **The Old Kingdom began with the Third Dynasty and ended with the Sixth Dynasty.**

The First Intermediate Period in Egypt
(2181–2055 BCE)

This chapter will explore the fascinating history of **the First Intermediate Period in Egypt,** which lasted **from 2181 to 2055 BCE.**
We will look at thirty interesting facts about this time that used to be seen as a **time of chaos.**

91. **The First Intermediate Period** lasted from 2181 to 2055 BCE.

92. **The ancient Egyptians** did not refer to this period as the First Intermediate; Egyptologists coined this term in the 19th century.

93. This period was once seen as **a time of political chaos and turmoil,** as Egypt was split into two main states, which were ruled by competing families.

94. It is not known for sure **why the kingdom split again**. Some historians believe that the long reign of Pepi II is to blame since he outlived his successors.

95. **The nomarchs,** local rulers, also had risen in power and become more independent.

96. Additionally, **the Nile was not flooding as expected**, leading to dry farmlands and famine.

97. **The Upper Kingdom was ruled from Thebes,** while the **Lower Kingdom was ruled from Heracleopolis**. There were other regions of power, but these were the two main bases.

98. During this period, **Egypt's central authority weakened**, and there were no powerful pharaohs to unite it again like before.

99. The First Intermediate Period is sometimes called **"the dark age"** of Egyptian history because very little is known about it compared to other periods like the Old Kingdom or the New Kingdom.

100. Scholars today believe that **the First Intermediate Period** was not a dark age as previously thought.

Ancient Egypt

101. The power no longer rested with a **central government**, which explains why huge monuments were not built during this time.

102. **Tombs were still built,** but they were not as grandiose as those built during the Old Kingdom.

103. **Coffin Texts,** which were texts painted inside coffins, were still used during the First Intermediate Period.

104. **The list of kings was not well documented** during this time, leading some to think it was a time of chaos. However, the power had shifted to local leaders, who continued to ensure their regions remained prosperous.

105. **Relations with other countries declined** somewhat, but trade continued as before.

106. The Egyptians also started using a new kind of irrigation system called **the shaduf** during this time, which allowed them to better control and regulate the flooding of their fields.

107. Historians believe the common misconception of **the First Intermediate Period** being a dark age has to do with how we tend to view history. In ancient Egypt, emphasis was placed more on the king and royal family instead of the common people.

108. The average person in Egypt did have to deal with a shift in politics, but **there is no evidence to suggest the people experienced poverty and chaos.** In fact, people of lower status were able to afford tombs during this period.

109. **Wealth no longer lay in the hands of just the elite,** allowing the common people to enjoy more luxuries.

110. **The First Intermediate Period** saw an increase in the quality of literature, giving rise to new genres in **the Middle Kingdom.**

111. The First Intermediate Period saw **a decrease in the quality of artwork,** though.

112. Part of the problem examining the artwork of this time lies with the lack of archaeological evidence. **It is possible this time saw advances in art that weren't recorded** by history.

113. **This period saw an increase in tomb robbery** due to the lack of a strong central authority in Egypt. Many tombs were plundered for their valuable items, such as jewelry and statues.

114. The First Intermediate Period encompassed **the Seventh to the Eleventh Dynasties**.

115. Not much is known about **the Seventh and Eighth Dynasties.**

116. According to ancient lists, **the Ninth and Tenth Dynasties each had nineteen rulers.** However, not much is known about their reigns.

117. **The first three kings** of the Eleventh Dynasty were **all named Intef.**

118. These rulers **helped create a sense of stability** and unity by defeating the nomarchs.

119. **Mentuhotep II,** who was a ruler during the Eleventh Dynasty, **unified the kingdoms again around 2055 BCE.**

120. **Mentuhotep II's tomb** was the first to associate the pharaoh **with Osiris,** the god of the afterlife and the dead.

The Middle Kingdom of Egypt
(2055–1650 BCE)

Delve into the rich history of ancient Egypt during **the Middle Kingdom**, which lasted from 2055 to 1650 BCE. This chapter will explore thirty interesting facts about their culture, beliefs, and art. Discover the advances they made in **mathematics, astronomy,** and **engineering** that allowed them to measure the height of buildings and create tools like plumb lines.

Learn more about pharaohs like **Amenemhat I, Amenhotep II, and Senusret II**. Uncover **the law code** they created, which included inheritance rights, marriage rights, and regulations regarding trade practices that would last for centuries.

121. **The Middle Kingdom of Egypt** was a period that lasted from 2055 to 1650 BCE.

122. During this time, ancient Egyptians were able to **rebuild and unite their country** after the First Intermediate Period, creating strong governance structures and laws that would last for centuries.

123. **Mentuhotep II,** who started the Middle Kingdom, made it clear that he had the divine right to rule and depicted himself as a god.

124. **Ancient Egyptians developed a taxation system** during this period that allowed them to fund public projects, such as building new monuments, temples, and other structures, that would last for centuries to come.

125. **The Middle Kingdom is also credited with creating laws** that were the first of their kind in ancient Egypt. Many important laws, such as inheritance rights, marriage rights, and regulations regarding trade practices, were written.

126. **Pharaohs during the Middle Kingdom** trained standing armies, which were used for defense and to obtain new lands.

127. **The Middle Kingdom is considered one of Egypt's most prosperous periods**. It saw significant advances in art, architecture, literature, and culture.

128. The Middle Kingdom period is also **well known for its tombs with elaborate artwork** that depicted everyday life in Egypt at the time.

129. **During this time, ancient Egyptians traded with neighboring countries** like Nubia and Palestine, allowing them to gain access to materials like gold, silver, and copper.

130. **Ancient Egyptians** developed more advanced sailing techniques during the Middle Kingdom, allowing them to explore lands outside their own borders and establish trade routes with other countries like Greece, Rome, and India.

131. **The Middle Kingdom period saw a significant influx of foreigners into Egypt,** such as Libyans, Nubians, Canaanites, and a small number of people from the Near East.

132. **Ancient Egyptian medicine** also made significant advancements during this time, as physicians could more accurately diagnose illnesses using methods like pulse readings and urine analysis.

133. **Pharaoh Amenemhat I** founded a new capital city at Itj-tawy around 1970 BCE.

134. The ruins of **Amenenhat's capital city have yet to be found,** so we don't know where this royal city was once located.

15

Ancient Egypt

135. **Amenemhat I appointed nomarchs** and required them to register their land to help curb their growing power.

136. **Ancient Egyptians used farming techniques** such as crop rotation, which helped increase food production levels without relying solely on the annual flooding of the Nile.

137. **Agriculture flourished** under various pharaohs of the Middle Kingdom, such as **Senusret III**, who built irrigation systems around the Nile Delta, allowing crops like wheat, barley, grapes, linseed oil, and cotton to be grown much more efficiently.

138. **Senusret III,** who ruled from 1878 to 1839 BCE, is considered to be the greatest king of the Twelfth Dynasty of the Middle Kingdom. He is known for his building projects, urban development, and expanding the kingdom to the south.

139. **Pharaoh Senusret III built several fortresses along Egypt's borders** with Nubia, which were used to defend Egypt against invasions from foreign forces.

140. **The Middle Kingdom** is also well known for its outstanding accomplishments in **mathematics, astronomy, and engineering.** Ancient Egyptians created tools like plumb lines to accurately measure the height of buildings.

141. **Pharaoh Amenemhat III,** who was part of the Twelfth Dynasty, built large mud-brick **pyramids at Dahshur and Hawara.** He was the first king since Sneferu (who was from the Fourth Dynasty) to build more than one pyramid.

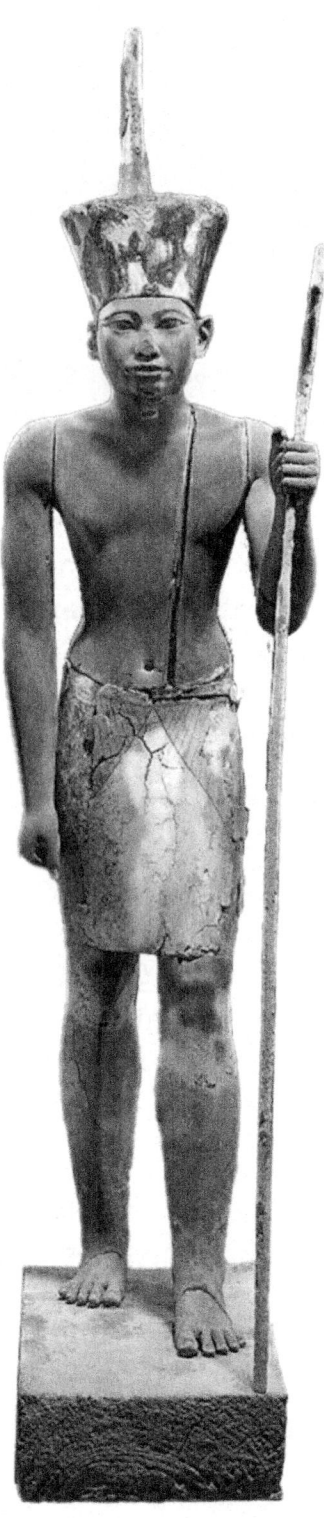

16

142. **Pharaoh Amenemhat III's tomb complex in Dahshur is known as the Black Pyramid.** It was the first pyramid to house the pharaoh and his queens. Before, queens had their own pyramids.

143. Also, during Amenemhat III's reign, one of the most famous works from ancient Egypt was written. **"The Story of Sinuhe"** is an epic poem about a man named Sinuhe who served under Pharaoh Amenemhat I, the founder of the Twelfth Dynasty.

144. **The Middle Kingdom** saw the continued worship of **the old gods,** such as **Sobek,** the crocodile god; **Seth,** the god of war and chaos; and **Khnum,** the god of the Nile and creation.

145. **Osiris became the most important god** during the Middle Kingdom.

146. **His popularity increased** because people outside of the royal family realized the afterlife could be attainable for them as well.

147. **The first female pharaoh, Sobekneferu,** ruled for almost four years during the Middle Kingdom Period.

148. **She was the last pharaoh of the Twelfth Dynasty.**

149. **Sobekneferu** was the first pharaoh to **associate with the god Sobek.**

150. **The Middle Kingdom** went from **the Eleventh Dynasty** (starting during the reign of Mentuhotep II) **to the Twelfth Dynasty.**

The Second Intermediate Period in Egypt
(1650–1550 BCE)

This chapter will explore the turbulent history of ancient **Egypt during the Second Intermediate Period.**
We'll look at thirty interesting facts about this era's **rulers and economy.** Join us as we discover this important period of ancient Egyptian history.

151. **The Second Intermediate Period** started around 1650 BCE and lasted until 1550 BCE.

152. **During this time, the Hyksos ruled Egypt**. However, other dynasties also ruled during this period.

153. The Second Intermediate Period encompassed several dynasties, beginning with **the Thirteenth Dynasty and ending with the Seventeenth.**

154. The Fifteenth Dynasty (**the Hyksos Dynasty**) ruled for most of the Second Intermediate Period.

155. No one is entirely sure **where the Hyksos originated from.** They probably came from the Levant. They gained a foothold in Lower Egypt.

156. **The Fifteenth Dynasty was the first time Egypt was ruled by a foreign power.**

157. **This period was once seen as a time of chaos** and upheaval in ancient Egypt. But like the First Intermediate Period, it is believed the Second Intermediate Period was not a dark age.

158. Some modern Egyptologists believe the **Hyksos didn't violently take over Lower Egypt,** which used to be the only theory on how they gained power.

159. From the evidence we have, it seems the **Hyksos admired the Egyptian culture;** they did not try to replace the traditional beliefs of the people with their own.

160. According to the peaceful takeover theory, the **Hyksos were attracted to Egypt** because of its prosperity. As time passed, more and more Hyksos moved to Egypt.

161. As **the Hyksos grew in power in Avaris**, a port located in the northeastern region of the Nile Delta, the Thirteenth Dynasty declined in power.

162. **The Thirteenth Dynasty** fled the capital of Itj-tawy and moved southward to Thebes.

163. When the Thirteenth Dynasty left, the **Hyksos were able to swoop in** and fill the power vacuum in Lower Egypt.

164. **The Fourteenth Dynasty** broke away from the Thirteenth Dynasty. Not much is known about either dynasty besides a few notable rulers.

165. Some believe the first few rulers of the Fourteenth Dynasty were **Canaanites** who declared their independence from the Thirteenth Dynasty.

166. **The Kingdom of Kush** (Nubia) grew in power during the Second Intermediate Period.

167. **The Nubians greatly admired the Egyptians,** adopting their gods, clothing, and even the way they acted with each other!

168. For a time, **the Hyksos and the Thebans** got along, although this would change during the Seventeenth Dynasty.

169. **The Hyksos ruled from Avaris.**

170. **The Hyksos built strong fortifications** around their cities to protect themselves from attacks by their enemies.

171. **The Hyksos rulers used their chariots and horses** to gain control over much of Lower Egypt during the Second Intermediate Period.

172. It is believed **the Hyksos introduced chariots to the ancient Egyptians.**

173. **When the Hyksos took over Memphis,** the royal family of the Thirteenth Dynasty fled south to the city of Thebes.

174. **The Sixteenth and Seventeenth Dynasties** ruled from Thebes.

175. **The Sixteenth Dynasty** lasted for around seventy years. Although it was short-lived, it was able to stop the Hyksos from advancing farther into its territory.

176. **Pharaohs Seqenenre Taa and Kamose** of the Seventeenth Dynasty led military campaigns against the Hyksos forces to restore control over Lower Egypt.

177. Their efforts ultimately helped **Ahmose I successfully reunite all of Egypt** under one ruler again.

178. **The Second Intermediate Period** was an important time in ancient Egypt's history. It marked a transition from foreign rule to unified control under one ruler again, setting up **the New Kingdom period.**

179. **The economy of Egypt** during the Second Intermediate Period was centered on agriculture and trade, with taxes being imposed on goods imported from other parts of the world.

180. **The Second Intermediate Period** was also a time of great cultural exchange between the different groups in Egypt, which resulted in a mix of Egyptian, Canaanite, and Near Eastern cultures.

20

The New Kingdom of Egypt
(1550–1070 BCE)

Explore the fascinating history of **the New Kingdom of Egypt,** which lasted from 1550 to 1070 BCE. **This was a period of great wealth and prosperity.** Discover thirty interesting facts about this period's culture, beliefs, and art.

Uncover the legacy of pharaohs like **Tutankhamun, Hatshepsut, Ramesses II**, and **Thutmose III,** who made outstanding contributions to the kingdom. And explore the literary works that provide insight into the social, political, and religious life of the period.

181. **The New Kingdom of Egypt** lasted from around 1550 to 1070 BCE.

182. **It was a period of great wealth** and prosperity in Egypt.

183. Military campaigns were launched to **expand the Egyptian kingdom** during this time, leading to victories over Nubia and Syria-Palestine.

184. Pharaohs such as **Tutankhamun, Hatshepsut, Ramesses II, and Thutmose III** ruled during this era of ancient Egypt's history.

185. **Queen Hatshepsut** was the second female pharaoh of Egypt. She made many contributions to the kingdom, such as sending diplomatic missions to Punt for trade and enlarging the religious complex at Deir el-Bahri near Luxor that still stands today.

186. **Thutmose III** transformed Egypt by leading seventeen successful military campaigns. He gained control of a large chunk of land.

187. **Pharaoh Amenhotep II** led several successful military campaigns against Nubia during his rule over Egypt, which led him to be remembered as one of the most powerful rulers from this era.

Ancient Egypt

188. **A new capital city called Amarna** was established during the reign of Akhenaten.

189. **Akhenaten sought to change Egypt's religion** by promoting a single god named Aten instead of the traditional polytheistic beliefs.

190. It is not known how **Akhenaten died, but his son, Tutankhamun**, rolled back his father's policies on religion.

191. **Nefertiti was married to Akhenaten**. Some believe she ruled after her husband's death. Her bust is one of the most well-known pieces of ancient Egyptian art.

192. **King Tutankhamun became famous for his tomb,** which was discovered by Howard Carter in 1922. Its many treasures lay intact, including the sarcophagus of the boy-king himself!

193. **Ramesses II is thought to be one of the greatest pharaohs in Egyptian history**. He conquered other nations in battle and built many monuments in Egypt, including the Ramesseum near Luxor, which was Ramesses's mortuary temple.

194. **The Hittites and Egyptians fought the Battle of Kadesh** in 1274 BCE, with both sides claiming victory afterward.

195. **The battle led to the first known peace treaty in history,** which was signed by the king of the Hittites and Ramesses II.

196. **Trade networks flourished** between Egypt, Nubia, Syria, Anatolia (Turkey), Greece, and Crete, which brought an influx of wealth into the country.

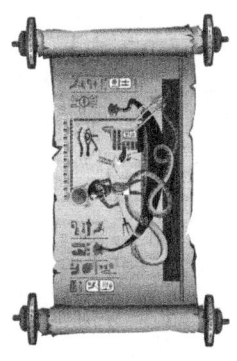

197. **The Egyptians traded papyrus paper, linens, gold,** and grain for wood, silver, copper, and cattle.

198. **Mummification was still practiced during this period** to preserve bodies for burial rituals.

199. **Embalming techniques were advanced** during this period, and mummies have been found that are over three thousand years old and still in excellent condition today.

200. **Elaborate tombs containing treasures like jewelry and amulets** made out of precious stones were also still created.

201. Instead of building giant pyramids, the pharaohs from the Eighteenth Dynasty to the Twentieth Dynasty were buried in **the Valley of the Kings**, located in modern-day Luxor.

202. During this period, **religious cults like Aten, Amun-Ra, Osiris, and Isis** rose to prominence within the kingdom. Festivals like Opet were held every year to celebrate the pharaoh, who was believed to be **the son of Amun-Ra.**

203. **Artisanship was highly esteemed.** Artisans used complex techniques to create beautiful gold and silver jewelry pieces. These artifacts can still be seen today, such as Tutankhamun's death mask.

204. **Music, dance, and theater were popular** forms of entertainment for commoners and royalty.

205. **Astronomical events like eclipses and solstices were studied and recorded** during this period, helping the Egyptians better understand their environment and how it affected them.

206. **The oldest known sundial in the world was created around 1500 BCE.** It was marked with hieroglyphics to indicate sunrise and sunset times.

207. **The twenty-four-hour day was invented during the New Kingdom.**

208. Literary works from ancient Egypt include **the Instruction of Amenemope,** which was a guidebook on how to live successfully.

209. **The Book of the Dead** was written during this period. It provided essential information on how to navigate the afterlife successfully.

210. **Literature from the New Kingdom** offered insight into social, political, and religious life. These pieces explored themes like gender roles, power dynamics, trade, and day-to-day activities, providing unique perspectives on the culture that archaeological evidence alone cannot.

Ancient Egypt

The Third Intermediate Period in Egypt
(1070–664 BCE)

The Third Intermediate Period of Egypt spanned from 1070 to 664 BCE and was a time of great cultural change. In this chapter, we'll explore thirty interesting facts about the Third Intermediate Period. Powerful military leaders, such as Shabaka, were essential in restoring Egypt's regional power.

211. **The Third Intermediate Period** in Egypt lasted from about 1070 to 664 BCE.

212. The Third Intermediate Period stretched **from the Twenty-first Dynasty to the Twenty-fifth Dynasty.**

213. During this period, foreign powers, such as **the Nubians and Libyans, ruled Egypt.**

214. Egypt was divided into two regions during this time: **Lower Egypt in the north and Upper Egypt in the south.**

215. **The Twenty-fifth Dynasty** is notable as it consisted of only Kushite rulers.

216. Although **the Twenty-fifth Dynasty was a line of Kushite pharaohs,** they did not change the Egyptian culture. The Kushites embraced Egyptian culture, as they used the Egyptian language and Egyptian artistic techniques.

217. A series of **royal tombs were built during this period at El-Kurru** near Sudan's border with Egypt. These Kushite tombs are some of the most important archaeological sites from this period in all of Africa.

218. **The Kushites built pyramids in the Nile Valley**; pyramids hadn't been built there for centuries.

219. **Tanis in the northeastern Nile Delta** became an important city during the Third Intermediate Period. It was the capital of the Twenty-first Dynasty.

24

220. **Shoshenq I founded the Twenty-second Dynasty.** The pharaohs of this dynasty came from a Libyan tribe.

221. **The Twenty-second Dynasty** overlapped with the Twenty-third Dynasty. These two dynasties saw a fall in Egypt's power.

222. **This period saw the use of Greek mercenaries** and the rise of influential military leaders, such as **Shabaka** and **Tefnakht.**

223. **Tefnakht founded the short-lived Twenty-fourth Dynasty.** He tried to restore power over Upper Egypt from his capital, Sais.

224. **Tefnakht formed the dynasty because Piye,** a Nubian king, sought to expand his control of Egypt.

225. **The Twenty-fourth Dynasty** came to an end when Shebitqo, the second pharaoh of the Twenty-fifth Dynasty, captured Sais.

226. **Piye was the founder of the Twenty-fifth Dynasty.** He ruled from Napata, which is located in modern-day Sudan.

227. **Shabaka was Piye's grandson.** His reign is notable because **he changed the capital** to Thebes and consolidated Kushite rule over Egypt.

228. **The Twenty-fifth Dynasty was large**, as it came to control Lower and Upper Egypt and Kush (Nubia).

229. This period also saw a lot of **cultural exchange between Egypt and other countries.**

230. **The Third Intermediate Period** saw increased Egyptian trade with other parts of the world, primarily through their ports on the Red Sea.

231. **Red Sea ports didn't access the Mediterranean back then,** although the Egyptians likely still traded with societies based in the Mediterranean during this period.

232. Some of **Egypt's most important trade partners** during the Third Intermediate Period were southern Persia and the lands south of Egypt in Africa.

233. During this period, **it was common for rulers to give land or gifts to their followers** to maintain loyalty. Some people even received plots of land from their kings.

234. The later part of this period saw the emergence of a **new type of writing known as Demotic,** which was used primarily for administrative documents and records throughout Egypt.

235. **Demotic writing became more popular during the Late Period**.

236. **The Twenty-fifth Dynasty** was pushed out by the Neo-Assyrians.

237. **The Assyrians installed Psamtik I on the throne of Egypt.**

238. **During Pharaoh Psamtik I's reign,** which lasted from 664 to 610 BCE, Egypt became more independent.

239. **Psamtik was able to gain help from the Lydians,** who sent Greek mercenaries.

240. **Psamtik and his successors were able to take control of Egypt again,** although they had to face more foreign threats in the future.

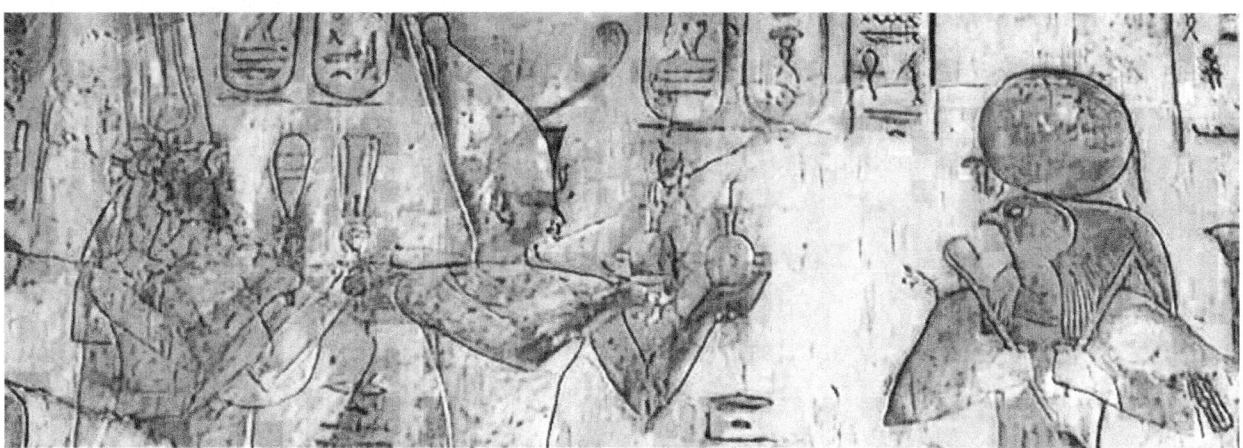

The Late Period in Egypt
(664–332 BCE)

This chapter will explore the fascinating history of ancient **Egypt during the Late Period.** We'll look at **thirty interesting facts about their culture,** as well as their advancements in medicine, trade, writing, and art.

With so much to learn, **let's dive into the exciting history** of the Late Period in Egypt.

241. **The Late Period in Egypt** lasted from 664 to 332 BCE.

242. **It was the last period of independent Egyptian rule** before it became subordinate to foreign empires.

243. **The pharaohs were still worshiped as living gods** at this time but had less power than they did in earlier periods due to foreign influence and the decline of governmental structures.

244. **The Twenty-sixth dynasty ruled from Sais in northern Egypt.**

245. **During this time, Egypt was ruled by foreign kings,** such as during the Persian takeover.

246. **The Egyptians were conquered by the Persians under Cambyses II** in 525 BCE.

247. **The Twenty-seventh Dynasty consisted of Persian emperors,** such as Xerxes I and Darius the Great.

248. During **the Twenty-seventh Dynasty,** Egypt was ruled as a satrapy, which means it was a province of the Persian Empire, not an empire of its own.

249. **Although the Persian emperors called themselves the pharaohs of Egypt**, the satrapy of Egypt was ruled by satraps or governors.

250. **The Twenty-eighth Dynasty had only one king, Amyrtaeus,** who ruled from Sais.

Ancient Egypt

251. **He rebelled against the Persians** but was overthrown by the founder of the Twenty-ninth Dynasty.

252. **The Twenty-ninth Dynasty was short-lived**, lasting for about twenty years.

253. **The Thirtieth Dynasty was the last dynasty of native rulers.** It lasted from about 380 to 343 BCE.

254. **The Persians again conquered Egypt**, starting the Thirty-first Dynasty.

255. **One famous pharaoh during the Late Period was Necho II,** who was part of the Twenty-sixth Dynasty. He **started to build a canal from the Nile River to the Red Sea.** He never finished it, but it is the first-known attempt at a canal connecting these two bodies of water.

256. **Under foreign rule, trade flourished between Egypt and other countries** like Greece, Rome, Syria, and Mesopotamia, bringing wealth to Egyptian cities.

257. **Egypt was a significant economic power,** exporting goods like linen, spices, and perfumes, among other items.

258. **The writing at this time shifted more towards Demotic Egyptian and away from hieroglyphs.** Demotic Egyptian was a cursive type of writing.

259. Art remained important during this period. **The Egyptians created realistic statues** and created works out of bronze, gold, and silver.

260. **Music also played an essential role** in daily life and religious ceremonies.

261. **Religious festivals were held throughout the year** in honor of different gods.

262. **Many gods were worshiped** during this period, including **Osiris** (the god of the underworld), **Ra** (the sun god), **Isis** (goddess of magic), **Horus** (falcon-headed god), **Bastet** (cat goddess), **Anubis** (jackal-headed god), and **Thoth** (god of knowledge).

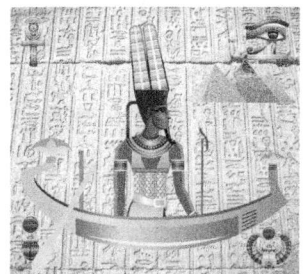

263. The most important god during this period was **Amun-Ra**, who was believed to be **a creator god**.

264. **Thoth also grew in importance during the Late Period.** For instance, millions of dead ibis were mummified near his cult center, Khmun.

265. **Mummification was still practiced** to preserve bodies for burial in tombs after death.

266. **Women had more rights in society** than in earlier times. They could even own property!

267. In **the Late Period, Egypt** was still a patriarchal society. Although **women had more rights in Egypt than in other ancient civilizations,** they didn't have much of a voice in how things were run.

268. **Medicine kept advancing in ancient Egypt**. The Brooklyn Papyrus, which dates to the Late Period, talks about magical and natural remedies for snakebites.

269. **The Late Period was a time of intellectual growth,** with scholars writing books on topics such as mathematics, astronomy, religion, and philosophy.

270. **The Late Period ended when Alexander the Great took over Egypt in 332 BCE.** Egypt became part of his empire.

The Persian Period in Egypt
(525—404 and 343-332 BCE)

This chapter will delve into the rich history of **the Persians of Egypt.** Since we have briefly touched on their rule above, we will focus on the Persian rule as a whole. Let's explore ten interesting facts about Persian rule.

271. **The Persian period in Egypt** actually consists of several dynasties: the Twenty-seventh Dynasty and the Thirty-first Dynasty.

272. **Persian kings ruled over much of the Middle East and North Africa, including Egypt** and parts of present-day Iraq, Iran, Syria, and Turkey.

273. **The Persians were known for their exceptional use of chariots in warfare.** They developed a highly organized army with a strict code of discipline, which was one of the reasons they were so successful in conquering other empires at the time.

274. **The Persians introduced a new type of governance known as a satrapy,** a decentralized government system where local governors, or "satraps," were appointed to govern over provinces while being subservient to the Persian king.

275. **Under Persian rule, Egyptians were allowed the freedom of religion** as long as they stayed loyal subjects. Many temples were built during this period, including those dedicated to gods such as Ra, Amun-Ra, Thoth, and Isis.

276. **The Persians developed an irrigation system called a qanat** to bring water from rivers into canals for agricultural and cooling purposes. Egyptians used this system until it was replaced by Roman technology, which allowed for better water control and distribution.

277. **During Persian rule, they introduced standardized weights and measures,** which allowed people to compare prices between cities or countries and **trade goods more accurately.**

278. **Persian rule introduced a new and more efficient system of taxation.** Taxes were collected from landowners throughout Egypt, which helped fund public projects like roads, bridges, and canals that improved transportation and communication.

279. **Persian rule of Egypt ended in 332. Alexander took over the region without having to fight a war!**

280. **Persian rule ended in 331 BCE** when the armies of Alexander the Great defeated them **at the Battle of Gaugamela.**

Alexander the Great in Egypt
(332–323 BCE)

This chapter dives into **the incredible history of Alexander the Great** and his reign over Egypt, which lasted from 332 to 323 BCE. We'll explore thirty fascinating facts about his life and the significant changes he implemented throughout **his time as pharaoh.** We'll uncover **how he spread Greek culture and improved life for Egyptians.** We will also explore how his legacy still lives today through the cities he founded.

281. **Alexander the Great was a king** of the ancient kingdom of Macedon.

282. **Alexander lived from 356 to 323 BCE.** At the age of twenty, he became king of Macedon after his father was assassinated in 336.

283. **His father, Philip,** was a pretty good leader as well. He conquered the Greek city-states shortly before his death.

284. **Alexander the Great is considered one of the greatest military commanders in history** and conquered much of the known world during his lifetime.

285. **In 332 BCE, Alexander led his army to Egypt** and took over the country without a war. **He was proclaimed pharaoh of Egypt.**

286. The Egyptian people proclaimed him to be the **incarnation of Ra and Osiris.**

287. Although **Alexander did not have to wage a war for Egypt,** he did face some trouble in Gaza.

288. **The commander of Gaza refused to surrender.** Gaza was heavily fortified at this time, so taking the city was no easy feat.

289. **It took Alexander four attempts to take the city.**

290. Once **Alexander conquered Gaza,** he allegedly killed all the men and enslaved all the women.

291. Perhaps it should not be surprising that Alexander won at Gaza. **It is believed that Alexander the Great never lost a battle.**

292. **He founded Alexandria in 331 BCE**, which became one of the most important cities in ancient times due to its strategic location on the Mediterranean Sea.

293. **This city is perhaps Alexander's most enduring legacy; the city is the second-largest in Egypt today.**

294. **Alexander spread Greek** culture in the lands he conquered. However, he respected local customs and did not try to change the people's beliefs.

295. For instance, **Alexander wore Persian clothing and married a Persian wife,** much to the chagrin of some of his generals.

296. **He wanted an educated population to keep his kingdom running smoothly.** Alexander created many schools that taught Greek culture.

297. **Although it took some time, Greek became a common language in Egypt,** especially among the ruling Greeks.

298. **Alexander the Great built one temple in Egypt, which he dedicated to Amun and Horus.**

299. **Alexander did not stay in Egypt for long.** Soon after founding Alexandria, Alexander moved on, never to return to Egypt.

300. **He left Egypt in the hands of the Egyptians,** which certainly further helped to endear them to him.

301. **Alexander would go on to conquer the Persian Empire in 331 BCE.**

302. **He wanted to conquer India as well.** Although he made it there, he was not able to conquer the Indian subcontinent.

303. **Alexander died at the age of thirty-two** after having conquered much of the known world from Greece to India.

Ancient Egypt

304. **It is not known for sure how he died. It is possible he was killed,** although it is also possible that he contracted malaria or another disease.

305. **Alexander the Great's wife, Roxana,** was pregnant at the time of his death. Although she gave birth to a son, he did not become king.

306. **Roxana and her son were killed sometime in 310 BCE.**

307. **After his death, his empire was divvied up by his generals.** These generals battled each other to try and earn more territory.

308. **It is not known where Alexander the Great's final resting place is.** It is likely he was entombed in Alexandria somewhere.

309. **His body was supposed to be buried in Macedonia,** but Ptolemy I Soter stole the body and had it interred in Memphis.

310. **The body was later moved to Alexandria.** It is not known if the body was moved again or where his tomb was located.

The Ptolemaic Period in Egypt
(305–30 BCE)

The Ptolemaic period in Egypt was a fascinating time that marked a significant change for the Egyptians and their culture. **The blending of Greek and Egyptian beliefs** and customs characterized this period.
We will explore **thirty facts about the Ptolemaic dynasty,** including its impact on trade, beliefs, and government.

311. **The Ptolemaic dynasty did not suddenly appear after Alexander the Great died. Ptolemy I first had to fight** for his part of Alexander's great empire.

312. **In 305 BCE, Ptolemy,** one of Alexander's generals, was able to solidify his hold over Egypt, creating a dynasty that would last until 30 BCE.

313. **Soter means "savior"** and was used by other pharaohs of this dynasty.

314. **Every male ruler of the Ptolemaic dynasty took the name Ptolemy.**

315. **The Ptolemaic pharaohs first ruled from Memphis** but later moved the capital to Alexandria.

316. **Alexandria became one of the most important cities in Egypt** during this period. It served as a hub for trade between Europe and Africa and was an intellectual center of learning and scholarship.

317. **Some famous scholars who studied in Alexandria include Euclid, Archimedes, and Eratosthenes.**

318. **The famous Library of Alexandria** was built by Ptolemy I Soter.

319. **The Great Library of Alexandria housed more than 400,000 scrolls**, making it famous throughout the ancient world.

320. **The Library of Alexandria burned during Caesar's time in the city.** He was trying to help Cleopatra in her war against her brother, and he burned some boats. The fire spread.

Ancient Egypt

321. It is believed the Library of Alexandria was rebuilt over this; it is not known for sure when it was destroyed for good.

322. The Ptolemaic dynasty oversaw a very robust trade with North Africa and East Africa.

323. Egypt became one of Rome's main suppliers of grain.

324. The Greek language became very popular. It was even written on new monuments during this period.

325. It is important to remember that **the Ptolemies were not Egyptian.** They didn't even speak Egyptian, **except for Cleopatra VII.**

326. Still, t**he Ptolemaic rulers respected the Egyptian culture** and even sponsored the construction of new temples.

327. Culturally, t**he Ptolemaic period was a time of blending between Greek and Egyptian beliefs** and customs.

328. **During this period, Serapis became a popular god**. He was a mesh of Greek (**Zeus**) and Egyptian (Osiris and Apis) deities. Serapis became very popular in Rome, although he did have a cult following in Egypt.

329. **The Rosetta Stone was carved during this period** and held three different scripts: ancient Greek, Demotic Egyptian, and Hieroglyphs. It later helped scholars decipher hieroglyphs.

330. **The Ptolemaic period saw the development of a complex bureaucracy in Egypt** that included tax collectors, military generals, and other government officials.

331. **The Ptolemaic period** was rather bloody. Even the famous **Cleopatra killed several of her siblings** to maintain power over Egypt.

332. **Cleopatra VII was the last ruler of Egypt from the Ptolemaic dynasty before it fell to Roman rule in 30 BCE.**

333. **During her reign, she allied with Julius Caesar** against her brother-husband's forces in a civil war that ended with her gaining control of Egypt.

334. **Incest wasn't popular in ancient Egypt,** but it did take place within the royal dynasty. The gods, such as **Osiris and Isis, married each other,** so it was a way for the ruling dynasty to connect more with the deities.

335. **After Caesar's assassination in Rome,** Roman general **Mark Antony allied with Cleopatra** against Julius Caesar's nephew and adopted son Octavian (Augustus).

336. **Mark Antony and Cleopatra's love story was famously written by William Shakespeare,** who certainly put a romantic flair on their relationship. However, the two likely did love each other very much and had children together.

337. **Cleopatra and Mark Antony were defeated** at the Battle of Actium in 31 BCE.

338. The two fled but were eventually **defeated by Octavian** the following year. **The lovers both chose to commit suicide** rather than face whatever Octavian had in store for them.

339. **Egypt fell under Roman dominion,** where it would stay for six hundred years.

340. Historians use **the Roman rule of Egypt** as a handy marker to indicate the end of ancient Egypt.

The Rise of the Pharaohs in Ancient Egypt

The story of the pharaohs is an incredible tale of power and influence that shaped the history of the ancient Egyptian civilization. We will explore ten fascinating facts about the pharaohs' rule and its impact on Egyptian society.

341. **The first dynasty of pharaohs began around 3100 BCE** during the time known as the Old Kingdom.

342. **The term pharaoh was not used until the New Kingdom;** before that point, the rulers simply referred to themselves as kings.

343. **Pharaohs were considered divine rulers.** They acted as intermediaries between the people and deities.

344. **Pharaohs were considered the most influential person in ancient Egypt;** their word was law.

345. **The position of pharaoh was hereditary,** so it was passed down from father to son or brother to brother.

346. **There were female pharaohs,** but they were not as common. **Hatshepsut** had such a hard time getting the people to accept her that she made her image appear androgynous.

347. It is believed that **170 different pharaohs ruled over Egypt.**

348. **The Great Pyramid of Giza** was one of the most impressive monuments built by a pharaoh; it took almost twenty years to build under King Khufu (r. 2589–2566 BCE). **The Greeks called Khufu** "Cheops."

349. **One of the most well-known pharaohs was Tutankhamun.** King Tut was around eighteen when he died, and his death is surrounded by controversy. He is well known today because of the discovery of his tomb.

350. **The last pharaoh of ancient Egypt was Cleopatra VII,** who reigned from 51 to 30 BCE. Her reign is notable for her civil war with her brother and her relations with famous Romans, such as Julius Caesar and Mark Antony.

Religion and Gods in Ancient Egypt

The religion of ancient Egypt is an integral part of this ancient civilization's rich history. We will explore ten facts about the **Egyptians' religion, gods, and goddesses**. These facts will give us a greater understanding of the gods and religion of ancient Egypt and their lasting legacy.

351. **The ancient Egyptian religion** was based on the idea that the gods controlled nature and the world around them.

352. **The Egyptians believed in many gods and goddesses,** most of which had human forms with animal heads.

353. **One of the most important gods for the Egyptians was Ra,** the sun god who also symbolized creation, rebirth, life, and death.

354. **The pharaohs were seen as divine,** as they had a connection to the gods. They were believed to have special powers from divine sources.

355. **Ancient Egyptians believed in the power of magic** and used it to protect themselves from evil spirits or bad luck.

356. **Egyptians used spells written in hieroglyphics** to summon spirits to help heal illnesses or find lost items.

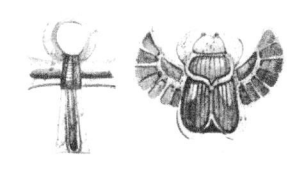

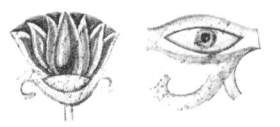

357. **The most famous symbol held by ancient Egyptian gods in art was the ankh,** which represents eternal life.

358. **The Eye of Horus was another religious symbol.** It was associated with protection against enemies and evil forces, good health, and prosperity.

359. Ancient Egyptians celebrated various festivals throughout the year in honor of their gods, such as the Festival of Osiris or the Festival of Bastet.

360. The ancient Egyptians believed in many different realms in the afterlife, which people went to depending on their actions while they were alive.

Pyramids and Tombs in Ancient Egypt

The pyramids and tombs created in ancient Egypt still inspire awe in us today and have captivated the imagination of people worldwide. We will explore ten facts about these **fascinating monuments**, such as what they were used for.

361. **The pyramids were tombs** for the pharaohs, the rulers of ancient Egypt.

362. **Egyptians believed the pharaohs needed their treasures** to be successful in the afterlife, so their tombs were filled with valuable items like gold, jewelry, and furniture.

363. **Tombs were often decorated** with beautiful art depicting scenes from ancient Egyptian life, as well as hieroglyphs telling stories about the deceased person's life and accomplishments.

364. **Some of these fascinating buildings** have been found underground beneath other structures, including temples or even cities; there may still be more waiting to be discovered.

365. **It was once believed that slaves built the pyramids,** but the general consensus today is that they were built by paid laborers.

366. **Pyramids have been studied for centuries** by scholars from all around the world, but to this day, **scholars still aren't sure how the pyramids were constructed.**

367. **Some tombs even had false walls or passageways** that led nowhere, making it difficult to find the actual entrance. These were put in place to make sure no one disturbed the body lying inside.

368. **The Step Pyramid of Djoser at Saqqara** was one of the first pyramids ever built. It stands just over two hundred feet.

369. **The Great Pyramid** is one of the most famous structures from ancient Egypt. It was built **by Pharaoh Khufu** about 4,500 years ago and stood at an incredible 481 feet. It is now around 450 feet tall.

370. **The most detailed and well-preserved tomb ever found was that of Tutankhamun,** who was only a teenager when he died around 1324 BCE.

Geography and Climate in Ancient Egypt

Geography and climate played a significant role in the history of ancient Egypt. We will explore ten facts about the geography and climate of this ancient civilization and discover the unique features that set it apart from other cultures.

371. **Ancient Egypt was located near the Mediterranean Sea** in the northeastern part of Africa.

372. **The climate in ancient Egypt was very hot,** dry, and sunny, with temperatures **up to 40°C** (104°F).

373. **Even today, Egypt receives very little rain** during the year.

374. **The ancient Egyptians relied on flooding from the Nile River** to water their crops each year.

375. **The Nile River flows south to north** and is the longest river in the world.

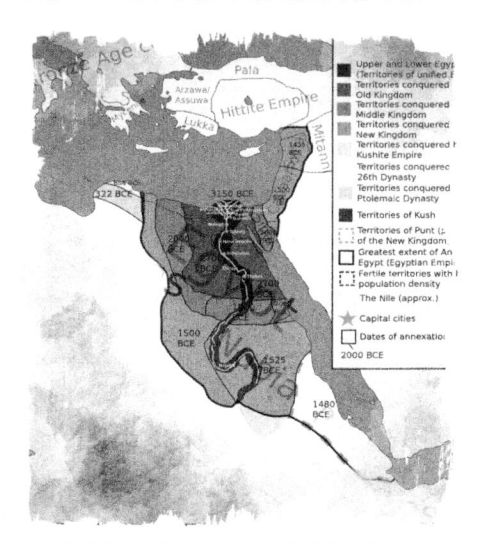

376. **The Egyptians built canals and dams** to help protect against floods and droughts. The canals transported water from one area to another when needed, while the dams stored floodwater in reservoirs during times of heavy rain.

377. **A unique feature of Egyptian geography is its deserts.** These arid lands cover more than 95 percent of the country's total area. In ancient Egypt, deserts served as natural barriers against invasion from foreign forces.

378. **The Sahara Desert is the largest desert in Egypt,** with temperatures reaching up to 47°C (117°F) during the summer months.

379. **Sandstorms are common occurrences,** with the storms sometimes lasting for weeks at a time.

380. **Lastly, ancient Egyptians relied on stars** to tell them when it was time for seasonal changes like sowing and harvesting crops and when to start sailing and trading along the Nile.

Writing and Hieroglyphs in ancient Egypt

Next, **we will explore ten facts about the writing system of ancient Egypt,** including **hieroglyphs** and **hieratic script**. The Egyptian writing system is one of the most well-known things about this ancient society, so let's learn a bit more about it!

381. **The ancient Egyptians** used a unique writing system called **hieroglyphs,** which **used pictures to represent words** and ideas.

382. **Egypt was one of four ancient societies to develop writing** independently.

383. **The earliest known examples of hieroglyphics date back to around 3400 BCE**, which was before the Old Kingdom.

384. In addition to being used in religious ceremonies and legal documents, **hieroglyphs were used to tell stories about gods and kings** from long ago.

385. **Ancient Egyptian scribes wrote with reed pens or brushes made from animal hair.** These writing implements would be dipped into black ink made from soot mixed with water or vegetable juice, such as onion juice.

386. **The ancient Egyptians wrote on papyrus paper,** which was made out of the stalk of the papyrus plant.

387. **The hieratic script is a cursive form of writing developed by the ancient** Egyptians and was used for everyday documents, letters, and records.

388. **Ancient Egyptians also wrote using hieratic numerals**, a system where numbers are written with symbols and not as we do today with digits (1, 2, 3, etc.).

389. **The Rosetta Stone is a famous stone tablet** written in three different scripts; hieroglyphic, Demotic Egyptian, and Greek.

390. **Although hieroglyphs can be found on the walls of tombs and pyramids,** no hieroglyphs were ever found in the Pyramids of Giza.

Government and Administration in Ancient Egypt

This chapter will explore **the government and administration of ancient Egypt.** We'll look at ten interesting facts about Egypt's government systems, laws, and nomes.

391. **Egyptian towns and cities were divided into administrative districts called nomes.**

392. **Each nome had a local government run by a nomarch,** who was responsible for collecting taxes and maintaining public services.

393. To keep track of citizens' whereabouts and activities, the **ancient Egyptians kept records of births, deaths, and marriages.**

394. **The Egyptian government imposed taxes** on goods imported from other countries.

395. **The ancient Egyptians had an extensive system of weights and measures** to calculate accurate prices for products being traded.

396. **This system included things like** measuring grain by the **hekat** (a unit equal to about five liters) or weighing gold by the **deben** (a unit equal to ninety-one grams).

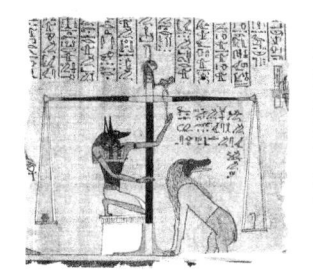

397. **The ancient Egyptians had a postal service**, which allowed them to communicate with other parts of the kingdom.

398. **People sent messages** via carrier pigeons or walking messengers known as heralds.

399. Some **Egyptian laws involved punishing** those who disobeyed orders from higher authorities (such as stealing) or protecting citizens' rights (like having access to clean water).

400. **Egyptian law was based on Ma'at**, their concept of justice. If Ma'at was out of order, then society would collapse.

The Military in Ancient Egypt

This chapter will explore ten fascinating facts about **the ancient Egyptian military.** We'll look at their ranks, weapons, tactics, and famous battles.

401. **Beginning in the Twelfth Dynasty, pharaohs created standing armies** to protect Egypt from nearby foes.

402. **The Egyptian army had an organized system of ranks and officers,** which helped them keep order on the battlefield.

403. **Military commanders** often wore bronze helmets decorated with a cobra or vulture to signify their rank and authority.

404. **Soldiers in ancient Egypt** were usually recruited from the lower class. Prisoners of war also fought as well.

405. **Ancient Egyptian soldiers** carried spears, swords, bows and arrows, slingshots, and bronze axes into battle.

406. **The biggest weapon in ancient Egypt's arsenal was an iron-throwing spear called a harpoon**, which could pierce through armor from faraway distances. These weapons were only available to wealthy individuals due to their high cost

407. In addition to weapons training, **men learned how to maintain discipline** by following orders without question, which was key to achieving victory over opponents.

408. **The ancient Egyptians had a navy,** which became highly advanced by the time of the Second Intermediate Period.

409. **They also used chariots pulled by horses** during battles to give them an advantage against enemies on foot. They would ride around enemy lines while shooting arrows at them. **Chariots played a very important role in ancient Egyptian battles.**

410. **Ancient Egypt's most famous battle** occurred between **Ramesses II and the Hittites** at Kadesh. Both sides eventually declared a truce after realizing neither had won decisively. This remains one of history's earliest recorded examples of diplomacy.

Economy and Trade in Ancient Egypt

Explore the economy and trade of ancient Egypt in this section. We'll discover ten interesting facts about how the Egyptians built an extensive trade network and **developed complex taxation systems**. We'll also learn how they traveled long distances.

411. **Egypt was a major economic player in the ancient world** and exported goods such as papyrus, linen, jewelry, oils, grains, and spices to other countries.

412. **The country also had a number of gold mines.** Miners were paid for their labor in wages and food rations. However, Egypt imported more gold than it mined.

413. **The Egyptians built boats from wood** and **tightly bound papyrus reeds**. They used boats to move goods between ports along the Nile River or across the Mediterranean Sea.

414. **Ancient Phoenicians from modern-day Lebanon traded with the Egyptians,** exchanging goods like wine, olives, and glassware for Egyptian wheat, linen, and silver coins.

415. **Trade between Egypt and other African countries** increased by the 13th century BCE as they exchanged spices, ivory, and precious metals.

416. **They also created an extensive network of trade** routes that allowed merchants to travel great distances through desert lands.

417. **By the New Kingdom**, Egyptian merchants **used camels instead of donkeys** to travel long distances over desert lands. They had to cross the hot sands when trading with distant cities like Damascus in Syria or Nubia (modern-day southern Egypt and northern Sudan).

418. **Merchants established trade guild**s that set standards for prices, quality, and quantity when trading goods with other countries or within Egypt.

419. **The pharaohs taxed landowners 10 percent of their harvest,** which they then redistributed among citizens who could not afford food during famine or drought.

420. **Egyptian rulers began taxing imported goods as early as 2500 BCE** to raise revenue to finance government projects like building monuments or preparing armies for war.

Ancient Egypt

Art and Architecture in Ancient Egypt

This chapter will explore **the fascinating art and architecture of ancient Egypt**. We will look at ten interesting facts about the structures they built, their statues and paintings, and their use of jewelry and precious stones.

421. **The Egyptians built some of the most magnificent structures in the ancient world,** including pyramids and temples.

422. **The Step Pyramid at Saqqara was Egypt's first monumental stone building**. It was constructed approximately around 2650 BCE.

423. **The Great Sphinx is one of Egypt's most famous monuments.** It guards the Pyramid of Khafre in the Giza Plateau.

424. T**hey used large stones for their constructions;** limestone blocks weighed, on average, over two tons each!

425. **The statues of rulers** were meant to last for eternity. They acted as a vessel for the spirit (ka) of a deceased king.

426. Although we are more familiar with the sculptures and statues that belonged to the elite, **the lower classes had statuettes placed in their tombs to serve as vessels for spirits.**

427. **Ancient Egyptians often decorated their tombs** with colorful drawings of people, animals, and plants.

428. **The Egyptians used five main colors** in their artwork: black, blue, gold, green, and red.

429. **Cats were often featured in Egyptian art.** The ancient Egyptians believed cats were sacred animals that protected them from pests like snakes and scorpions.

430. **Ancient Egyptian jewelry** was made **from precious stones** like lapis lazuli and gold. Colored glass beads were also used.

Literature and Poetry in Ancient Egypt

This chapter will explore the captivating literature of ancient Egypt. We'll uncover ten fascinating facts about their use of words to express stories, emotions, beliefs, and history

431. The earliest known story in ancient Egyptian literature is **"The Tale of Two Brothers,"** which dates back to around 1200 BCE. T**his story talks about kingship and the divinity** of the pharaoh.

432. **Ancient Egyptian literature** was also used to record history and tell stories, such as the famous epic poem "The Story of Sinuhe."

433. **Poetry was an important form of expression in ancient Egypt.** Poems were used to tell stories or express emotions like love, joy, and sadness.

434. **Ancient Egyptian poets** were known to have written about the beauty of nature and their love for life.

435. **One type of poem from this period was funeral dirges,** mournful songs sung for those who had passed away.

436. Other famous forms of ancient **Egyptian poetry include hymns to the gods, proverbs, and riddles.**

437. One example of **ancient Egyptian poetry is called Instructions of Amenemhat,** which was written during the Middle Kingdom. The "Instructions" are just that, instructions from a ruler to his son in the form of a poem.

438. **Ancient Egyptians believed that reading and writing poetry could be magical.** It could bring things into existence and heal people's illnesses.

439. **The gods and goddesses in ancient Egypt** were often featured in poems. They were usually depicted as powerful yet benevolent figures.

440. **Poetry was thought to be a way** for people to connect with the gods and goddesses.

Science and Technology in Ancient Egypt

This chapter will explore **the ancient Egyptians' incredible science and technological achievements.** We'll look at ten interesting facts about their **mathematics, engineering, and astronomy.** We'll also discover how the ancient Egyptians developed complex **systems to measure time** and utilized the natural environment to their advantage.

441. **Ancient Egyptians were some of the first people to use medicine,** advanced **mathematics,** and **engineering** for everyday life.

442. **They invented a number system** based on multiples of ten, which was later used by other civilizations like Greece and Rome.

443. **They also created tools for measuring,** like scales, rulers & plumb lines – some have been discovered inside ancient temples too.

444. **The pyramids in Egypt are one of the most impressive ancient structures.** Although it is not known for certain how they were built, building them required complex mathematical equations so their sides would be aligned.

445. **Astronomy was very important** to the ancient Egyptians. They kept track of time by using groups of stars called decans.

446. **The ancient Egyptians** were the first to create a sundial, allowing them to use the sun to tell time.

447. Before this, **obelisks were used to tell the time** based on the shadow of the sun.

448. **Glass-making was another skill** developed during this period; glass objects, such as mirrors, beads, and amulets, have been found in many tombs. Although they were not the first to create glass, they perfected their techniques to create stunning works.

449. **Ancient Egyptians were the first to use a simple form of plumbing.** They used clay pipes (and later, copper pipes) to move water from one place to another.

450. **The Egyptians built ships with sails** made out of linen so that they could travel down rivers or make lengthy voyages on the Mediterranean or Red Sea.

Social Structure and Roles in Ancient Egypt

This chapter will explore **ancient Egypt's social structure.** We'll take a look at ten interesting facts about their classes, education, women's rights, and entertainment.

451. **People in ancient Egypt were divided into two main classes.** There was the wealthy and privileged **upper class,** who had access to better resources. **Lower-class citizens** lived off what they could get from working hard jobs without much return other than necessities like food and shelter.

452. **Priests were very powerful** and oversaw religious ceremonies and rituals.

453. **Scribes were also important.** They wrote down laws or essential information, such as royal decrees or tax records, on papyrus scrolls using **a brush called a reed pen.** The pen would be dipped in ink made from soot mixed with water or honey-based glue.

454. **Farmers worked the land along the Nile River.** They grew wheat, barley, and other crops, which provided food for Egyptians and trade with other nearby countries.

455. **Merchants traded goods with other civilizations.** The land of Punt was one of ancient Egypt's most important trading partners. **The exact location of Punt is still unknown,** but it was based somewhere in the Red Sea region.

456. **Artisans made jewelry from gold and silver** using tools like hammers and saws to cut stones into shapes. Potters used clay to make vessels for storing liquids or cooking food over fire pits outdoors.

457. **Education was mainly available only to the wealthy classes,** as they could afford tutors to teach their sons how **to read and write** and solve math problems. **Lower-class children would be taught at home.**

458. **Women had fewer rights** than men but still played an essential role in society by managing households, taking care of children, and spinning thread out of the flax plant. **Women in ancient Egypt had more rights than other ancient civilizations.**

459. **Music was popular among Egyptians,** whether listening to professional musicians play instruments at festivals or singing songs during religious ceremonies dedicated to the gods.

460. **Entertainment was an essential part of life for people during this time.** Ancient Egyptians enjoyed **board games** and **outdoor sports.** The earliest form of **bowling** can be traced back to ancient Egypt!

Clothing and Appearance in Ancient Egypt

This chapter will explore the fascinating **history of clothing in ancient Egypt.** We'll look at ten interesting facts about the **materials, designs, jewelry, makeup, and hygiene** practices of the time.

461. **Although ancient Egyptians wore colorful clothing.** However, toward the beginning of the ancient Egyptian civilization, **they primarily only wore white linen.**

462. **Wealthy people's clothes were made from fine linen** or other expensive materials like silk.

463. **Men wore dresses similar to kilts called schenti**, with pleats in the front and long sashes at the waist.

464. **High-ranking women usually wore a sheath dress,** which was tight around their waists but loose below so they could move easier when walking or dancing.

465. **Older people** were considered wiser in ancient Egypt, so they often **chose traditional clothing styles** over more modern ones to demonstrate their wisdom.

466. **Most people dressed according to their social class,** which was a way to distinguish between the wealthy and the poor.

467. **Upper-class men and women wore jewelry,** such as necklaces, earrings, bracelets, anklets, wigs, and headdresses, to show off their wealth or religious beliefs.

468. **All ancient Egyptians wore jewelry,** which was used to denote one's status. For instance, **gold could only be worn by kings, royals, and priests.**

469. **Ancient Egyptians often wore makeup**, such as **kohl** (black eyeliner) and **rouge** (red powder applied to cheeks).

470. **Most people bathed regularly. The poor would bathe in the Nile,** while **the elite would bathe inside.** Ancient Egyptians also wore a **perfume** made from flowers or spices.

Farming and Agriculture in Ancient Egypt

This chapter will explore the intricate farming and agricultural techniques used by the ancient Egyptians. We'll look at ten interesting facts about their **crops, tools, livestock, and techniques** used to ensure successful **harvests.**

471. **Ancient Egyptians grew emmer, barley, and garlic as staples of their diet.**

472. **They used a plow called an ard** to break up soil for planting crops in the Nile Valley.

473. **Farmers used animal dung from cows and buffalo** to fertilize their fields before they planted new crops.

474. **Ancient Egyptian farmers** often used simple machines like levers and pulleys to lift heavy loads more easily.

475. **Ancient Egyptian farmers were skilled at building canals** and irrigation systems to help with crop growth and avoid drought-related losses due to a lack of water supply during dry seasons.

476. **Ancient Egyptian farmers kept records of their harvests by counting the grain and writing it down in a ledger.** This helped them **keep track** of how much they produced each year so they could plan for future needs or any potential shortages.

477. **Fishing along riverbanks was an important activity** that contributed significantly toward nourishment during different times, although **Egyptians fished year-round.**

478. **Beekeeping was also practiced in ancient Egypt.** Honey was prized for its healing properties and used to make food tastier. **It was often eaten with bread during meals**.

479. **Goats, sheep, and poultry were all popular livestock animals in ancient Egypt**; their wool could be spun into fabric, while chickens provided eggs and meat protein sources.

480. **Ancient Egyptians also kept cats and dogs around their farms and homes** to keep pests away from the crops. This helped ensure that any insects or rodents **didn't contaminate the food** they produced.

Medicine and Health in Ancient Egypt

This chapter explores **the remarkable medical practices of the ancient Egyptians.** We will delve into ten interesting facts about their treatments, tools, and discoveries. Explore how they used their knowledge **of anatomy and physiology to heal the sick and protect against disease.**

481. **Ancient Egyptians believed the human body was made up of five elements** that had to be balanced for good health.

482. **The ancient Egyptians used medicine as part of their religious practices,** including spells, rituals, and offerings to gods or goddesses that were thought to protect against disease.

483. **Doctors used a variety of herbs and minerals** in treatments like poultices, salves, and drinks.

484. **Ancient Egyptian doctors could perform necessary surgeries** like **setting broken bones** and **stitching open wounds** using tools made from stone and copper alloyed with tin.

485. **Ancient Egyptians made casts or molds from wax, plaster,** and linen to stabilize broken bones until they healed.

486. **Ancient Egypt** is credited with having some advanced medical knowledge, such as recognizing t**he importance of washing hands before performing operations** and being able to diagnose some illnesses through physical examination alone.

487. **Ancient Egyptians also regularly washed and bathed,** although they did not do this for medical reasons. They believed that the cleaner a person was, the happier the gods would be.

488. **Ancient Egyptians cleaned their teeth** using sticks rubbed against them while they had a daily bath or shower.

489. **Ancient Egyptians discovered how blood circulated around the body** much earlier than Europeans did. This knowledge is attributed to **Imhotep,** who wrote extensively on anatomy and physiology **during the Old Kingdom**.

490. **Ancient Egypt gave us the world's first written medical text known** as **the Edwin Smith Papyrus,** a fifteen-foot scroll containing forty-eight cases of trauma and diagnosis with suggested treatments. **Edwin Smith purchased the scroll in Egypt in 1862,** and it's now in the Metropolitan Museum of Art in New York City.

Death and Burial in Ancient Egypt

This chapter will explore **the ancient Egyptian beliefs about life after death** and how their **burial practices** were designed to ensure a **safe journey into the afterlife.** We'll take a look at ten interesting facts about **mummification,** burial ceremonies, and more.

491. **Ancient Egyptians believed life after death** was just as important as life on earth.

492. **Ancient Egyptians believed the dead would be judged by the god Osiris.** If they were found worthy, their soul would go to a place called the **Field of Reeds or Aaru,** an eternal paradise without any hardships or sadness.

493. **After a person died, their body was carefully preserved** in a process called **mummification,** which removed all moisture from the body so that it wouldn't decay over time.

494. **Ancient Egyptians believed that the heart was needed for life after death,** so it was left inside the body when mummified. The other internal organs would be removed.

495. **A body undergoing mummification** would go through a ritual known as the **opening of the mouth,** which they believed would allow the body to speak, eat, and drink again in the afterlife.

496. **Mummies were wrapped in many layers of linen cloth** and **placed inside a sarcophagus.** Sarcophagi weren't unique to Egypt, but mummies and sarcophagi are some of the most enduring symbols of ancient Egypt.

497. **Burial ceremonies usually included singing, dancing, and offerings of food** and drink to help accompany the deceased into the afterlife.

498. **The tomb or burial place was often decorated with artwork,** statues, and religious symbols. They believed these images would come to life and aid the deceased in their journey to the afterlife.

499. **Pharaohs had huge tombs filled with treasures,** such as gold jewelry, furniture, and other items needed for their afterlife.

500. **Ancient Egyptians strongly believed in an afterlife,** so much so that even those who were not wealthy or powerful still enjoyed elaborate burials with their personal belongings.

Conclusion

The story of ancient Egypt stretches back **thousands of years**, from the dawn of humanity to its conquest by **Alexander the Great**. Its legacy is as vast and impressive as it was powerful, filled with incredible achievements in art, architecture, literature, and science. It has left a wealth of **knowledge about its religion, government, military power, and economy. In this book,** we have learned about clothing styles, farming practices, and social roles.

Ancient Egypt continues to influence cultures around the world today, and many appreciate its contributions to humanity, including **monumental architectural** feats that still stand today, **hieroglyphic symbols** that are studied, scientific advances, and so much more. **Ancient Egypt was a remarkable civilization,** and its legacy will likely be celebrated forever.

As we come to the end of **our exploration of ancient Egypt**, we cannot help but feel a sense of awe and **admiration for all this great civilization** has left behind. From its prehistoric origins to **the rise and fall of the pharaohs,** ancient Egypt has left us with a lasting legacy in the form of religious beliefs, art, and literature. **This legacy is a source of inspiration** for us all as we strive to learn more about our past to create a better future.

Sources and Additional References

Fagan, Brian M. Ancient North Africa. Oxford University Press, 2016.

Shaw, Ian, and Paul Nicholson. The British Museum Dictionary of Ancient Egypt. The British Museum Press, 1995.

Edwards, I. E. S. The Cambridge Ancient History. Cambridge University Press, 1982.

Baines, John. "Egyptian Writing and Art." In Ancient Egypt: Art, Architecture, and History, edited by Lawrence Berman and Carlotta Stern, 83–106. Los Angeles: Getty Publications, 2007.

Wilkinson, Richard H. The Complete Gods and Goddesses of Ancient Egypt. Thames & Hudson, 2003.

Simpson, William Kelly. Ancient Egypt: A Social History. Cambridge University Press, 2001.

Taylor, John H., and N. de Garis Davies. The Tomb of Nefertari. London: British Museum Press, 1985.

Hornung, Erik. The Ancient Egyptian Books of the Afterlife. Cornell University Press, 1999.

Redford, Donald B. Ancient Egypt: A Social History. Cambridge University Press, 1984.

Strudwick, Nigel. The Encyclopedia of Ancient Egypt. Oxford University Press, 2005.

Silverman, David P. Ancient Egypt. Oxford University Press, 2003.

Baines, John, and Jaromir Malek. The Cultural Atlas of Ancient Egypt. Penguin, 2000.

Quirke, Stephen G. Ancient Egyptian Religion. London: British Museum Press, 1992.

Brier, Bob. Ancient Egyptian Magic. New York: William Morrow, 1980.

Robins, Gay. The Art of Ancient Egypt. Cambridge, MA: Harvard University Press, 1997.

Redford, Donald B. Akhenaten: The Heretic King. Princeton, NJ: Princeton University Press, 1984.

Assmann, Jan. The Mind of Egypt: History and Meaning in the Time of the Pharaohs. Cambridge, MA: Harvard University Press, 2003.

Wilkinson, Toby. The Rise and Fall of Ancient Egypt. Bloomsbury, 2010.

Ions, Veronica. Egyptian Mythology. The Rosen Publishing Group, 2002.

Kemp, Barry J. Ancient Egypt: Anatomy of a Civilization. Routledge, 2006.

Redford, Donald B. Egypt, Canaan, and Israel in Ancient Times. Princeton University Press, 1992.

Hornung, Erik. Conceptions of God in Ancient Egypt: The One and the Many. New York: Cornell University Press, 1996.

Shaw, Ian. The Oxford History of Ancient Egypt. Oxford: Oxford University Press, 2000.

"The Old Kingdom." Encyclopedia Britannica, Encyclopedia Britannica, Inc.

"The Age of the Pyramids." Encyclopedia Britannica, Encyclopedia Britannica, Inc.

"Hieroglyphics." Encyclopedia Britannica, Encyclopedia Britannica, Inc.

"Ancient Egypt." Encyclopedia Britannica, Encyclopedia Britannica, Inc.

"Egyptian Mythology." Encyclopedia Britannica, Encyclopedia Britannica, Inc.

Joyce, William A. The Ancient Egyptians. New York: Oxford University Press, 2013.

Smith, Mark. The Great Pyramid: Ancient Egypt Revisited. Cambridge: Cambridge University Press, 2004.

Smith, Grafton Elliot. The Ancient Egyptians: Their Life and Customs. London: Macmillan, 1910.

Spalinger, Anthony. War in Ancient Egypt: The New Kingdom. Oxford: Blackwell Publishing, 2005.

Redford, Donald B. The Ancient Gods Speak: A Guide to Egyptian Religion. Oxford: Oxford University Press, 2002.

Redford, Donald B. The Oxford History of Ancient Egypt. Oxford University Press, 2003.

Wilford, John Noble. The Mapmakers: The Story of the Great Pioneers in Cartography from Antiquity to the Space Age. Vintage Books USA, 2000.

Faulkner, Raymond O. The Ancient Egyptian Pyramid Texts. Oxford University Press, 2016.

Assmann, Jan. The Search for God in Ancient Egypt. Cornell University Press, 2001.

Printed in Great Britain
by Amazon